Mariah Carey

Judy Parker

HIGH
interest
books

Children's Press
A Division of Scholastic Inc.
New York / Toronto / London / Auckland / Sydney
Mexico City / New Delhi / Hong Kong
Danbury, Connecticut

To Coy, Donna, and Karen who were all almost born on Mariah's birthday!

Book Design: Michael DeLisio
Contributing Editor: Eric Fein

Photo Credits: Cover © Sean Roberts/The Everett Collection; pp. 4, 18, 25, 36 © Mitchell Gerber/Corbis; p. 7 © Nader Group International, Randy Nader/Corbis; pp. 8, 13, 16, 26, 31, 34 © The Everett Collection; p. 11 © Carraro/Stills/Retna Ltd.; p. 15 © Steven White/Retna Ltd.; p. 21 © Bill Davila/Retna Ltd.; p. 22 © Steve Granitz/Retna Ltd.; p. 33 © Frank Micelotta/Retna Ltd.; p. 39 © Keibun Miyamoto/Retna Ltd.

Library of Congress Cataloging-in-Publication Data

Parker, Judy.
    Mariah Carey / Judy Parker.
    p. cm. — (Celebrity bios)
    Includes bibliographical references and index.
    ISBN 0-516-23425-0 (lib. bdg.) — ISBN 0-516-29600-0 (pbk.)
    1. Carey, Mariah—Juvenile literature. 2. Singers—United States—
    Biography—
Juvenile literature. [1. Carey, Mariah. 2. Singers. 3. Women—Biography. 4.
    Racially mixed people—Biography.] I. Title. II. Series.

ML3930.C257 P37 2001
782.42164'092—dc21

                                                                00-066047

CONTENTS

CHAPTER ONE

An Amazing Woman

"I've always been 100% driven to do this," she says of stardom. "Every minute of my life."

–Mariah in *Time* magazine

Mariah Carey is the best-selling female singer in history. Ten years ago, Mariah was an unknown backup singer. Today, she has sold more than 120 million albums worldwide. This is her inspiring story.

MULTIRACIAL ROOTS

Mariah Carey was born on March 27, 1970, on Long Island, New York. Mariah's mother,

When well-dressed Mariah appears at award shows, people notice.

Patricia, was an opera singer. She also worked as a vocal coach. Her father, Alfred, was an engineer.

Mariah is multiracial. She is a mix of white, African-American, and Hispanic. Her background played a big part in how she saw herself as she grew up. Before she was born, Mariah's parents had to deal with a lot of prejudice. Some people didn't like their multiracial marriage. Patricia Carey was white and Irish Catholic. Alfred Carey was African-American and Hispanic.

> **Did you know?**
>
> Patricia Carey began giving voice lessons to Mariah at the age of three.

Some people treated the Careys badly. This forced the family to move. The stress of being a mixed couple was too much for them. Patricia and Alfred divorced.

Mariah had her difficulties growing up. Yet she has never
forgotten her Long Island roots.

Singing helped Mariah deal with her troubles as a young woman.

Mariah didn't face the same kind of discrimination as her parents. Still, she felt different. "I always felt like an outsider," she told *InStyle* magazine. "Partly because I'm multiracial and partly because of not having much money when I was a kid."

Mariah was three years old when her parents divorced. She lived with her mother and her older brother and sister. Mariah's mother had a hard time making ends meet. The family moved all over Long Island as Patricia tried to find a good job.

Patricia worked hard to make a living as a singing teacher. During this time, she realized that Mariah also had a gift for singing. "From the time Mariah was a tiny girl, she sang on true pitch; she was able to hear sound and duplicate it exactly," Patricia told *People* magazine.

SCHOOL DAYS

In high school, Mariah wrote songs of her own. She sometimes worked with Ben Margulies, a musician friend of her brother. Music was what Mariah cared about most.

Writing her own songs helped her deal with her feelings. Mariah loved to listen to pop and soul singers, such as Diana Ross and Aretha Franklin. She also enjoyed jazz singers, such as Sarah Vaughn and Billie Holliday. Rhythm and blues and rap were the biggest influences on her music.

A LUCKY BREAK

Mariah graduated from high school in 1987. After graduation, she moved to New York City. She was determined to start her singing career. Mariah checked coats and waitressed. In her spare time, she recorded a demo tape. A demo tape is a sample recording. Singers often record their songs on demo tapes. They then send these tapes to record companies. The songs on Mariah's demo tape included "All in Your Mind," "Someday," and "Prisoner."

Mariah continued to support herself with odd jobs. She then had a lucky break. Singer Brenda K. Starr needed a background singer. Mariah got the job. "Brenda was very support-ive, like a big sister, and she used to bring me shoes and coats and things when I didn't have any money," Mariah told MTV.

Soon, Mariah's work with Brenda K. Starr paid off. At a party for Columbia Records in

Performer Brenda K. Starr gave Mariah her first big job. She hired Mariah as a background singer.

1988, Starr helped get Mariah's demo tape to Tommy Mottola. Mottola was in charge of finding new talent for Columbia Records. On his way home from the party, he listened to the demo tape. He loved what he heard. Mottola was sure that he had found the next Whitney Houston.

Mottola went back to the party to look for Mariah, but she had left. He tracked her down the next week and offered her a record contract. "He left a message on my machine," Mariah told *People* magazine in 1993. "I called back, stuttering: 'Can I speak to M-Mister M-Mottola?' He said, 'I think we can make hit records.' I was like freaking out!"

Did you know?

Mariah has so many clothes that she has to number them so she doesn't wear the same outfit twice.

In 1988, Columbia Records told Mariah they wanted to sign her to a contract. Mariah couldn't believe her great luck!

IN THE STUDIO

Mottola and Mariah took more than a year to prepare for her first album. Mariah wanted to produce the album with her songwriting partner, Ben Margulies. Mottola wanted her to work with more experienced producers. He hired people who had worked on some of Whitney Houston's biggest hits.

Mariah co-wrote eleven songs. They were all on the finished album. Margulies helped write six of the songs. Mariah produced one song,

"Vanishing," by herself. It was a beautiful, gospel-based song.

The album was set to be released in June 1990. Mottola made sure that all the right people heard it before then. Mariah gave a special concert at a convention for national record store owners in Los Angeles. She then sang on a private tour for radio station executives. Mariah's talent amazed people. By the time the album was released, she had important fans in the music business. All of them were eager to present her to the public.

A HUGE SUCCESS

Two months after it was released, *Mariah Carey* went platinum. The album sold one million copies. It was number one on the *Billboard* charts. It stayed at number one for twenty-two weeks. Four songs from the album became number-one hits. They were "Vision of Love,"

Here, Mariah sings one of the hits from her first album.

"Someday," "Love Takes Time," and "I Don't Wanna Cry." Eventually, *Mariah Carey* sold more than nine million albums.

Mariah's first album was a huge success with the public. Even the music critics liked it. The *Chicago Tribune* wrote, "Mariah's voice can probably shatter glass and then put it back together."

CHAPTER TWO

Mariah's Career Takes Off

"I went into this phase of recording, recording, recording and doing it really fast."

—Mariah in *Time* magazine

By January 1991, *Mariah Carey* sold more than three million copies. In February, sales continued to go up because Mariah won two Grammy Awards. The Grammy Awards are the music industry's highest honors. Mariah won for Best New Artist and Best Female Pop Vocal Performance for the song "Vision of Love." By April, sales went through the roof. *Mariah*

In the chilliest months of 1991, Mariah's record sales heated up.

Critics and fans were dazzled by Mariah's first album. Every week, it seemed she won another award.

Carey sold more than five million copies in less than a year.

The awards kept coming. Mariah won three Soul Train Music Awards, an American Music Award, and several *Billboard* Music Awards. She returned to the studio to record her second album, *Emotions*.

WORKING WITH THE BEST

Mariah took more control of her second album. She wanted a lighter sound. Mariah also wanted to experiment with different musical styles, such as rhythm and blues and jazz. She chose Robert Clivilles and David Cole to produce her dance songs.

Clivilles and Cole had a successful band of their own called C & C Music Factory. They produced their band's huge dance hit, "Gonna Make You Sweat." Mariah turned to Walter Afanasieff for the ballads on *Emotions*. Afanasieff produced some of the songs on Mariah's first album.

Mariah co-wrote the lyrics for all ten songs on *Emotions*. She wrote songs with her producers. Mariah also worked with singer and songwriter Carole King. King was famous for writing the songs "You Make Me Feel Like a Natural Woman" and "You've Got a Friend."

King's *Tapestry* was a best-selling album in the 1970s. King enjoyed working with Mariah. She spoke with *New York* magazine about the experience. "It was a true collaboration. In the end we came up with what we both think is a wonderful song." The song, "If It's Over," was a sad ballad. Mariah's vocals were recorded in an unusual way. She sounded like a one-woman gospel choir.

Emotions was released in September 1991. Mariah's winning streak continued. The songs "Emotions" and "Can't Let Go" both hit the top ten. *Emotions* sold more than two million copies worldwide in only three months.

LOVE FINDS MARIAH

As Mariah settled into her new life, she fell in love with Tommy Mottola. From the moment they met, Mottola focused all of his energy on Mariah. He was determined to make her a big

Love soon blossomed between Tommy Mottola and Mariah.

success. Mariah fell in love with him because of his dedication. "I can't imagine anybody else who would be so supportive and so understanding and helpful," Mariah told *People*. "He lifts me up."

Mottola was nineteen years older than Mariah. He also was married. In June 1990, he separated from his wife. During this time,

Mariah is used to hanging out with stars. Here, she and Tommy pose with TV legend Dick Clark (far right).

rumors started about Mariah and Mottola. Mariah told *People*, "There is not much that is sacred in this business, but to me, my private life is." In October 1991, Mariah was engaged to Mottola.

PRESSURE TO PERFORM

By 1992, Mariah was a superstar. She was only twenty-one years old, but already she had two hugely successful albums. People expected her to go on tour. Instead, Mariah went back into the studio to record her third album.

At this point, people thought that Mariah was afraid to perform publicly. "I'm something of an introvert," she told *The New York Times*. "I'm happiest when I'm creating in my own little world in the studio. I'm not into performing." Yet the pressure grew for Mariah to perform for her fans.

Around this time, MTV launched a concert series called "Unplugged." Musicians who appeared on "Unplugged" did not use electric musical instruments. MTV invited Mariah to perform. She agreed. It was one of the best professional decisions she ever made.

On March 17, 1992, Mariah performed for the "Unplugged" audience. The fans in the room loved what they heard. One of the songs was The Jackson Five's "I'll Be There." She performed it as a duet with backup singer Trey Lorenz. After the show aired, "I'll Be There" was released as a single. The song was a hit. It moved quickly to the top of the charts. It stayed at number one for four weeks straight.

In June 1992, Mariah's amazing concert on "Unplugged" was released as an album. It took only one month for the album to go platinum. Best of all, Mariah proved that she could perform in concert for her fans.

WEDDING BELLS

Tommy married Mariah in the summer of 1993. The wedding was a big event and drew attention from all over the world. The wedding cost almost half a million dollars. Many celebrities and musicians attended. Barbra Streisand, Billy Joel, and even Ozzy Osbourne were among the guests.

Mariah wore an ivory gown by designer Vera Wang. The gown had a 27-foot-long train. It had to be carried by six ladies in waiting.

Tommy and Mariah had what seemed to be a fairy-tale wedding.

Mariah's veil was the same style as the one worn by Princess Diana in her wedding. After the honeymoon, the couple lived in a huge mansion in Bedford, New York.

"Every day I count my blessings," Mariah told *People*. "I mean, I'm this poor kid from Long Island and now this!"

On MTV, Mariah finally gave fans what they wanted: a live concert.

THE ARTIST GROWS

Mariah's third album was *Music Box*. It was released in August 1993, two months after her marriage to Mottola. Three more singles reached number one: "Dreamlover," "Hero," and "Without You." Mariah also began a small U.S. tour in late 1993. This time the critics were not kind to her. Mariah still was not comfortable performing live. She couldn't make things perfect the way she could in the studio. Yet the public loved her. By June 1994, *Music Box* had gone platinum seven times over.

When she wasn't touring, Mariah was at home in Bedford. She spent many hours in her home recording studio. She worked on two albums, *Merry Christmas* and *Daydream*. She did not give many interviews. When she did, she sounded happy. Things were changing, though. Mariah was growing both as a woman and as an artist. She wanted to act. She also wanted more rhythm and blues and rap in her songs. She was going through big changes. There was no going back.

Did you know?

Mariah was the surprise guest performer at the National Multiple Sclerosis Society's Dinner of Champions in 1999. She sang "Hero." She missed the MTV Awards to go to the benefit.

CHAPTER THREE

The Butterfly

"I feel more free to put more of myself into my music. There's a lot of real emotion in Butterfly. I lived with it. I woke up to it."

–Mariah in *Time* magazine

In October 1995, Mariah's album *Daydream* was released. Even the critics liked it. *Time* magazine said, "*Daydream* is her best album yet." Once again, Mariah had multiple number-one hits, including "Fantasy" and "Always Be My Baby." The album was nominated for several Grammy Awards in 1996. Unfortunately for Mariah, Alanis Morissette's *Jagged Little Pill* swept the awards.

Still, Mariah had the number-one song of the year for 1996. Her duet with the group Boyz II Men, "One Sweet Day," stayed at number one for a record-breaking sixteen weeks.

TOUR AND DREAMS

In 1996, Mariah went on a world tour to promote *Daydream*. She no longer was nervous about performing live. Quietly, Mariah pursued acting. There were rumors that her need to try new things caused trouble in her marriage. "Tommy and I have a great relationship," she told *Time*. "Like anyone, we have to work things through."

By 1997, Mariah's marriage was on the rocks. In May, Mariah and Mottola announced that they were separating. Mariah moved into her own apartment in Manhattan. It was a difficult situation. By this time, Mottola was the head of Sony Records. Mariah was the record label's biggest-selling artist.

Mariah fired her manager and her lawyer. They both were friends of Mottola. She hired Sandy Gallin. Gallin managed singer Dolly Parton and actress Nicole Kidman. Mariah tried to be her own person. Yet even after their marriage ended, she and Mottola stayed on friendly terms.

NEW DREAMS

Mariah explored new interests. She hired an acting coach. She told *Entertainment Weekly*, "My whole life I've wanted to act." Eventually, her determination paid off. In 1999, she had her first small film role. She played an opera singer in the movie *The Bachelor*, starring Chris O'Donnell. It was a great start. Yet Mariah wanted to make a movie that showed her own struggles to become a successful artist. In time, she would find a way to make that dream come true, too.

Mariah made her acting debut in the movie *The Bachelor*.

Mariah started branching out musically. She tried a hip-hop sound for her next album, *Butterfly*. Sean "Puffy" Combs produced the first single, "Honey." Mariah co-wrote the song "Babydoll" with rapper Missy "Misdemeanor" Elliott. Mariah also recorded dance remixes for clubs. They featured guest rappers such as Mase and Da Brat. Mariah even co-wrote and produced more ballads with Walter Afanasieff.

ON TOP

Butterfly was released in September 1997. By October, the album had gone double platinum.

The song "Honey" hit the number-one spot on the charts. The song "Butterfly" hit number two. Both songs were nominated for Grammy Awards, but Mariah did not win. Album sales were still strong in June 1998. That was when the single "My All" went to number one.

Did you know?

After her separation from Tommy Mottola, Mariah lived in a townhouse that was used in the film *The First Wives Club.*

The video for "Honey" combined Mariah's new musical sound with her new life as a single woman. In the video, Mariah played a female secret agent. She was held prisoner by a wealthy

Mariah belts out a crowd-pleasing hit from the album *Butterfly*.

man in a mansion. She fought bad guys, wore designer clothes, and rode a Jet Ski. Some people thought that the video made fun of her ex-husband. "It's not intended to be a dis to Tommy," she told *Entertainment Weekly*. The video was nominated for an MTV Video Music Award.

In the summer of 1998, Mariah took everyone by surprise when she recorded a duet with Whitney Houston. People thought that the singers would be enemies because they worked

Mariah turned some heads when she sang with Whitney Houston.

for different record companies. The duet with Whitney was for the soundtrack to the movie *The Prince of Egypt*. The song "If You Believe" hit the top ten when it was released in late 1998. Mariah told MTV, "Whitney was just really cool and we had a really good time in the studio. We had fun, and it was a good experience."

RUMORS AND ROMANCE

Mariah's new lifestyle kept her working late into the night and sleeping during the day. She spent time with friends at New York City nightclubs. Many of her friends were hip-hop music artists. Rumors began to fly about her new life. "It was ridiculous," Mariah told *Time*. "There were rumors and lies about me being the next queen of gangsta rap, which did not help."

Mariah met New York Yankees shortstop Derek Jeter at a charity benefit in 1997. They started dating in 1998. Mariah and Derek had a lot in common. They both came from multiracial marriages. She told *InStyle*, "His mom is Irish and his father's black—same thing as me. I had never met anybody like that, and that's always been a big part of who I am." Dating someone else famous was not easy. Reporters followed their every move. It was hard for them to find time together. They both had demanding careers. Eventually, Derek and Mariah's relationship ended.

Mariah makes a point of giving money and time to charities.

MAKING HISTORY

Mariah finished the 1990s with hit after hit. She released *#1's*, an album with all of her number-one singles as well as some new songs. She was featured in the VH1 *Divas Live* concert in October 1998. The CD from the concert was also a hit.

Mariah recorded *Rainbow*, a new album released in late 1999. She made history when the first single, "Heartbreaker," hit number one on the charts. She had songs in the number-one spot for a total of sixty weeks. This broke the Beatles' record of fifty-nine weeks.

FROM THE HEART

For ten years, Mariah's life has centered on her amazing recording career. Now, she makes time for other things. Mariah supports charities that are important to her. One of the most important is Camp Mariah, the Career Awareness camp. It is run by the Fresh Air Fund. The camp is for twelve- to fourteen-year-old kids from low-income families in New York City. There is more to Camp Mariah than just outdoor fun. Kids work on projects that develop leadership skills and self-esteem.

Mariah also gives back to the communities where she grew up. In October 1999, she returned to her old high school in Greenlawn, New York. She gave a surprise concert for the students and teachers. She talked with the students and signed hundreds of autographs.

THE SILVER SCREEN

Mariah continues to act. Her work in *The Bachelor* was well received. She auditioned for the role of Natasha in *The Adventures of Rocky and Bullwinkle*. Mariah didn't get the part, but she didn't give up. She finally produced and starred in a movie based on her own life, *All That Glitters*. Mariah also co-wrote the movie.

All That Glitters was filmed in the summer and fall of 2000. It stars Mariah as a woman struggling to make a life as a singer. She also has a difficult time with her husband. Her co-stars include singer Eric Benet and rapper Da Brat.

INTO THE FUTURE

As Mariah moves forward, it will be exciting to see how she faces her future challenges—both

Mariah is a woman who knows what she wants out of life.

professional and personal. She already has achieved great success because of her talent and hard work. Mariah knows what is important in her life. "What really matters at the end of the day is not how many records I've sold," she told *Entertainment Weekly*. "I know who I am."

TIMELINE

1970	• Mariah Carey is born on March 27.
1987	• Mariah graduates from high school and moves to New York City.
1988	• Tommy Mottola gets Mariah's demo tape at a party.
1990	• In June, the album *Mariah Carey* is released. • In August, *Mariah Carey* goes platinum.
1991	• Mariah wins two Grammy Awards. • In September, *Emotions* is released. • In November, *Emotions* goes double platinum.
1992	• In June, Mariah releases *MTV Unplugged*. • In July, *MTV Unplugged* goes platinum. • In December, Mariah wins two *Billboard* Music Awards.

TIMELINE

1993   • In June, Mariah marries Tommy Mottola.

1994   • In June, Mariah releases *Music Box*.
           • Mariah releases *Merry Christmas*.

1995   • In October, *Daydream* is released.
           • In December, *Daydream* goes quintuple platinum.

1997   • In May, Mariah separates from Tommy Mottola after almost four years of marriage.
           • In September, *Butterfly* is released.

1998   • In August, Mariah and Whitney Houston record the duet "When You Believe" for the movie *The Prince of Egypt*.
           • Mariah appears on VH1's *Divas Live*.

1999   • In November, *Rainbow* is released.
           • In December, Mariah receives the Artist of the Decade Award at the *Billboard* Music Awards.

TIMELINE

2000	• Mariah receives an Award of Achievement at the American Music Awards. • Mariah is honored as Best-Selling Female Pop Artist of the Millennium at the World Music Awards.
2001	• Mariah signs a multi-million dollar record deal with Virgin Records.

FACT SHEET

Name	Mariah Carey
Nickname	Mirage
Born	March 27, 1970
Birthplace	Long Island, New York
Family	Mother: Patricia; Father: Alfred; Brother: Morgan; Sister: Allison
Sign	Aries
Height	5'9"
Hair	Brown
Eyes	Brown

Favorites

Actor	James Dean
Actress	Marilyn Monroe
Movies	*The Color Purple*
Pets	Five dogs: Jack (Jack Russell terrier), Princess (Doberman), Ginger (Yorkshire terrier), and Bing and Bong (shih tzus)
Color	Pink
Singer	Aretha Franklin
Food	Lemon Chicken

NEW WORDS

audition to try out for something

charity an organization that helps people

chart a listing that ranks music sales

demo tape a music recording made for a
   record company

discriminate show an unfair difference toward
   people or groups

duet a song for two performers

ethnic relating to a racial, national, or
   cultural group

gospel a type of music that celebrates Christianity

Grammy Award an award given in honor of
   musical achievement

hip-hop music that features breaks, samples of
   songs, and rap

mansion a large house

multiracial involving different races

opera a theatrical work often set to classical music

platinum record certificate awarded to a record
   that sells one million copies

pop relating to popular music, as in "pop chart"

NEW WORDS

prejudice unfair dislike of a person or a group based on race or religion

producer the person who supervises the production of a record, film, or television program

rhythm and blues (R&B) music that includes elements of blues and African-American folk music

rap a form of speaking in rhyme, often with a hip-hop beat

soul music that started with African-American gospel singing

soundtrack the music recorded for a movie

studio a place where a record or CD is recorded

FOR FURTHER READING

Nickson, Chris. *Mariah Carey Revisited: Her Story*. New York: St. Martin's Press, 1998.

Shapiro, Marc. *Mariah Carey*. Toronto: ECW Press, 2001.

Wellman, Sam. *Mariah Carey (Galaxy of Superstars)*. Pennsylvania: Chelsea House Publishers, 2000.

RESOURCES

The Official Mariah Carey Web Site
www.mcarey.com
Mariah's Sony Web site includes all the latest information. Mariah contributes interview clips at regular intervals.

The Official Mariah Carey Fan Web Site
www.mariahcarey.org
The official Mariah fan site is a great resource for all things Mariah!

The Fresh Air Fund
www.freshair.org
The homepage of Mariah's favorite charity. It has information on Camp Mariah.

INDEX

About the Author

Judy Parker has written on a variety of subjects for young adults. She is a Latin music fan and loves to dance salsa.